CONFLICT RESOLUTION
Solving Your People Problems

JUNE HUNT

AspirePress

Torrance, California

CONTENTS

Definitions.. 8
   What Is a Conflict?..................................... 9
   What Is the Difference between
      Resolution and Reconciliation? 11
   What Are Types of Conflict? 13
   What Is God's Heart on Conflict
      Resolution?... 16
   Who Creates Conflict and Who
      Keeps It Going? 19

Characteristics of
Dysfunctional Conflict.............................. 25
   What Are Common Statements
      Used in Conflict? 26
   What Do Attackers and Avoiders
      Look Like?.. 28

Causes of Conflict 38
   Why Are Some People Attackers
      and Others Avoiders? 39
   What Are the Unmet Needs That
      Drive Attackers and Avoiders? 42
   What Causes the Worst Conflict? 46
   Root Cause of Negative Conflict 50

Steps to Solution 52
   How to Respond When Others Are
      Critical of You 56
   The What, Why, and How of Boundaries......... 59
   Recipe for Conflict Resolution 63

How to Respond to Difficult Personalities 67

The Road to Resolution... 71

Why Should I Forgive When the
  Conflict Is Not Resolved? 76

How Do You Keep Forgiving
  Following a Major Conflict?............................ 78

What Will Protect Your Heart
  from Bitterness? 81

ear Friend,

Are you afraid of conflict? In your vocabulary, does the word "conflict" spell—t-r-o-u-b-l-e?

When you hear the word "conflict," what do you picture? A fighting family? A feuding friendship?

I'll have to admit, when I hear the word "conflict," my natural tendency is to do *anything to avoid it*! Yet as I think about the serious conflicts I've had in my life—my most difficult relationships—I see times of *greater personal growth* than if the conflicts had not existed.

And because of these difficult relationships, I became aware of lessons I needed to learn, not only about others, but more importantly, about needed changes in my own attitudes and actions. Had everything been peaceful, I honestly do not believe I would have stretched my ways of thinking or changed as I needed to change.

Years ago I heard this insightful statement, "Never to be angry, never to disagree at all seems to most of us a sign not of love but of indifference."

We, obviously, live in a world of differences. You are not identical to anyone. Your background, even within your family, will be different from a brother or a sister because you are in a different birth order.

Even if you were an identical twin, you would have been born with a different temperament;

people would be interacting with you differently. Inevitably, you would have *differences of opinion*.

And, of course, these differing opinions are the breeding ground for conflict. Be aware, if you are an "avoider" of conflict (like I have been), that will also bring on conflict. So if we can't avoid conflict, what are we to do?

The answer is not to be an avoider—a "peace at any price" person—to let people have their way. (I've changed from this ... I really, really have!) Neither is the answer to be an "attacker," to have it "my way." The solution is not *retreating* or *reacting* but *responding* to conflict appropriately.

And why is this important? So that you can live with right priorities, experience personal growth, and display that deepest peace—the peace that passes all understanding.

My prayer is that, through these pages, you will not only learn different ways of dealing with conflicts, but that, most of all, you will become the person God created you to be.

Yours in the Lord's hope,

June

June Hunt

"I have never yet known the spirit of God to work where the Lord's people were divided."

—D.L. Moody

CONFLICT RESOLUTION
Solving Your People Problems

Living in obscurity as a Jewish orphan, she seemed the least likely candidate to be the mediator—the only mediator—to possibly save her people from sure destruction. However, the Lord knew her heart, and He knew she would face the most severe conflict of her life with complete humility.

The entire conflict arose because of conniving Haman, a royal official in the king's court, who devised a plot to murder every Jewish person in the empire. His fury had been flamed by a man who refused to bow down to him—namely, Esther's cousin Mordecai, who had raised her. Little did Esther know that she would carry the fate of the Jewish people on her shoulders as she faced a conflict of epic proportions. Yet Mordecai aptly posed ...

"Who knows whether you have not come to the kingdom for such a time as this?"
(Esther 4:14 ESV)

DEFINITIONS

Just how does Esther, this unknown young woman, become queen? After days of feasting, King Ahasuerus (King Xerxes) is "merry with wine" and wants to show off the beauty of his wife before the people and nobles. He summons seven attendants to send for her. However, Queen Vashti refuses to come. The king becomes enraged.

At the advice of his closest counselors, the king issues a royal decree: Queen Vashti can never again enter into the king's presence, and she will be replaced! (Esther 1:19). With this new edict, the outward conflict between the king and queen appears to be "resolved." But the resolution of one conflict sometimes gives rise to another—now the king has no queen. And because of the queen's haughtiness, the king's advisors felt they had to take action or else throughout the land.

> "There will be no end of
> disrespect and discord."
> (Esther 1:18)

In order to avoid discord and conflict among the people, a major search ensues. All the beautiful young virgins in the land are rounded up so that "*the girl who pleases the king*" would be selected as queen (Esther 2:4). Esther, described as a young woman who "*was lovely to look at*," quickly gains favor. At cousin Mordecai's instruction, she does not reveal her heritage. After a full year, Esther is finally taken to the king and he, "*loved Esther more than all the women … and made her queen instead of Vashti*" (Esther 2:17 ESV).

The plan for alleviating the loneliness of the king puts Esther on the path of God's divine purpose— but also on a collision course with a conflict of colossal proportions.

▶ *Conflicts* are disagreements, struggles, or battles over opposing issues or principles.[1]

▶ *Conflictus*, the Latin word, means an "act of striking together or clashing with."[2]

▶ *Conflict*, in Greek, is often the word *agon*,[3] from which the English word "agony" is derived. Originally meaning a "place of conflict," this word came to mean the actual conflict itself and later any kind of conflict, struggle, or strife. The apostle Paul said, "*I want you to know how much I am struggling for you and for those at Laodicea, and for all who have not met me personally.*" (Colossians 2:1)

Now a personal power struggle begins when corrupt Haman, the top royal official, becomes infuriated with Mordecai, who day after day refuses to bow down to him.

Meanwhile, wise Mordecai uncovers a plot that ultimately saves the king's life. Haman is so outraged that, when he discovers Mordecai is a Jew, he manipulates getting a royal decree from the king mandating the massacre of all the Jews—every man, woman, and child. Haman has won the conflict. He will get his homage, but at a very high—and *horrific cost.*

"When Haman saw that Mordecai would not kneel down or pay him honor, he was enraged. Yet having learned who Mordecai's people were, he scorned the idea of killing only Mordecai.
Instead Haman looked for a way to destroy all Mordecai's people, the Jews, throughout the whole kingdom of Xerxes."
(Esther 3:5–6)

At this point, no positive resolution is possible. The king's decree has sounded. However, Mordecai appeals to Esther for help. She can't believe what Mordecai is asking her to do. He knows the law: *"Any man or woman who approaches the king in the inner court without being summoned the king has but one law: that he be put to death."* (Esther 4:11)

Since she has not been summoned by the king for 30 days, how can she go to the king to plead on behalf of her people? What if the king becomes displeased with her? She needs to be reconciled to the king. Clearly, going to the king will mean putting her life on the line. To which Mordecai responds that her life is on the line either way!

> "Do not think that because you are in the king's house you alone of all the Jews will escape. ... And who knows but that you have come to royal position for such a time as this?" (Esther 4:13–14)

Resolution vs. Reconciliation

Resolution and reconciliation are different.

▶ *Resolution* means "finding the answer," derived from the Latin *resolutionem*, "the process of reducing things into simpler form" or "to lessen."[4]

▶ *Reconciliation* means "100% restoration to harmony"; "to bring together again."[5]

Some differences may never be resolved, but you can still be reconciled to those with whom you differ. At other times, resolution may be possible, but reconciliation inappropriate—such as in the case of adultery or cult entrapment—God requires only that, as far as it is possible, you seek to be at peace with everyone.

> "Aim for perfection ... be of one mind, live in peace. And the God of love and peace will be with you."
> (2 Corinthians 13:11)

QUESTION: "Is forgiveness the same as reconciliation?"

ANSWER: No. Forgiveness is not the same as reconciliation. Forgiveness focuses on the offense, whereas reconciliation focuses on the relationship. Forgiveness requires no relationship, while reconciliation requires nurturing a relationship—a time of coming together in which two people, in agreement, are walking together toward the same goal. The Bible says,

> "Do two walk together unless they have agreed to do so?"
> (Amos 3:3)

All of a sudden, Esther is facing an *inner conflict* just as heavy, just as grave, just as deadly as the *outer conflict* caused by Haman.

On multiple levels, Esther is a conflicted soul. Where will she find the strength, the courage, to do what must be done?

1. *Intra*personal Conflict

- A struggle **within oneself** to decide between two or more choices.

- In the book of Esther, does Esther approach the king in an attempt to save the Jewish people from extinction—which could earn her a death sentence—or does she remain silent and live? Esther said,

  "All the king's officials and the people of the royal provinces know that for any man or woman who approaches the king in the inner court without being summoned the king has but one law: that he be put to death. The only exception to this is for the king to extend the gold scepter to him and spare his life. But thirty days have passed since I was called to go to the king." (Esther 4:11)

2. *Inter*personal Conflict

- A clash of ideas or interests **between two or more people**.

- In the book of Esther, malicious Haman plots to have Mordecai murdered only because Mordecai refuses to bow down to him.

"When Haman saw that Mordecai would not kneel down or pay him honor, he was enraged." (Esther 3:5)

3. *Intra*organizational Conflict

- A competitive or opposing action **within a group** (a family, department, church, political party, state, or nation).

- In the book of Esther, the king learns about the plot which was crafted—not by the enemy on the outside—but by Haman, his top official on the inside. The king becomes enraged after realizing Haman has manipulated him into issuing a death sentence to murder all the Jewish people.

"The king got up in a rage, left his wine and went out into the palace garden. ... So they hanged Haman on the gallows he had prepared for Mordecai. Then the king's fury subsided." (Esther 7:7, 10)

4. *Inter*organizational Conflict

- A battle or opposing action **between two or more groups** (families, companies, religions, or countries).

- In the book of Esther, because of Haman's surreptitious plot, the Persian nation threatens to annihilate the entire Jewish population—men, women, and children.

"Dispatches were sent by couriers to all the king's provinces with the order to destroy, kill and annihilate all the Jews—young and old, women and little children—on a single day, the thirteenth day of the twelfth month, the month of Adar, and to plunder their goods." (Esther 3:13)

Conflict abounds in the book of Esther, just as conflict fills the pages of our lives. The "should I" or "shouldn't I's," disharmony in the home, wars in the workplace, all try us and ought to lead us to the One to whom Esther will turn for the strength, courage, and resolution she needs. His name isn't even mentioned in the entire book of Esther, but His sovereignty spreads itself like a shadow over every chapter.

Drastic times call for drastic measures.

Esther asks Mordecai to gather all the Jews in Susa, one of the empire's main capitals, and have them all fast for her. Three entire days of no food and no drink, and she and her maids will do the same. Esther enlists the people of God to pray for rescue, *for resolution of the most formidable challenge of her life.*

"Go, gather together all the Jews who are in Susa, and fast for me. Do not eat or drink for three days, night or day. I and my maids will fast as you do. When this is done, I will go to the king, even though it is against the law. And if I perish, I perish." (Esther 4:16)

Her act of faith worked to open his heart. When she approaches the king without having been summoned, he extends to her the golden scepter of grace. Now she is allowed to make her request. When Esther invites the king and Haman to a banquet that day, the king seems eager to fulfill her wishes.

After the king and Haman attend the feast, Esther invites them to a second feast the next day. On this day she will plead the case on behalf of her people.

In the middle of the feasts, Haman is crafting gallows 50 cubits high (75 feet) on which to have Mordecai hanged! But while Haman is building, the king orders that the book of memorable deeds during his reign be read to him. Found within its pages is the account of Mordecai's having saved the king's life. The following morning as Haman arrives at the palace to talk about hanging Mordecai, the king asks him, *"What should be done for the man the king delights to honor?"* (Esther 6:6)

Confident the king must be referring to him, Haman proposes placing royal robes and a crown on the man and having a noble official lead him on one of the king's horses through the city square, proclaiming, *"This is what is done for the man the king delights to honor!"* (Esther 6:9)

While Haman is indeed part of the king's plan, his role is beside the horse, not on it! Humiliated, Haman leads Mordecai, mounted on a steed, through the city streets—for all to see. Then, entirely mortified, Haman returns home after the public spectacle. There he receives from his wife and friends a message not of hope, but of doom: *"Since Mordecai, before whom your downfall has started, is of Jewish origin, you cannot stand against him—you will surely come to ruin!"* (Esther 6:13)

▶ Conflicts can be used to accomplish God's purpose. (Only after becoming queen was Esther able to save the Jewish nation.)

"We know that in all things God works for the good of those who love him, who have been called according to his purpose." (Romans 8:28)

▶ Conflicts cannot always be avoided.[8] (Esther and the Jewish people could not escape Haman's threats.)

"I have told you these things, so that in me you may have peace. In this world you will have trouble. But take heart! I have overcome the world." (John 16:33)

▶ Conflicts are not necessarily bad. When handled well, they provide an opportunity for role modeling. (For centuries, Esther has been and continues to be a role model of how to make an appeal to a higher authority.)

"As iron sharpens iron, so one man sharpens another." (Proverbs 27:17)

▶ Conflicts require action toward peace. (Esther had to take action in order to save her people.)

"Let us therefore make every effort to do what leads to peace and to mutual edification." (Romans 14:19)

▶ Conflicts require advance preparation and planning. (Esther meticulously planned two royal dinners, the timing of her petition, and her very words.)

"Prepare your minds for action; be self-controlled; set your hope fully on the grace to be given you when Jesus Christ is revealed." (1 Peter 1:13)

▶ Conflicts can be settled through negotiation. (Esther graciously negotiated with the king.)

"Listen to advice and accept instruction, and in the end you will be wise." (Proverbs 19:20)

The next day, during the second feast, at the king's urging, Queen Esther finally makes her request that her people be spared from annihilation by the crafty snake, Haman (Esther 7:3–6). Not only does the king grant her request, but in his rage he has Haman hanged on the very gallows he had built for Mordecai.

After a time of great conflict, true resolution resonates throughout the land for the Jewish people. But none of this would have happened if Esther had *avoided* the conflict (retracting herself like a turtle). Instead, she confronted the conflict and rose to the occasion, *"for such a time as this."* (Esther 4:14)

THREE ATTACKERS: Outwardly Aggressive

1 Wolves

Wolves are fierce, savage, and cruel animals that make a terrible howling sound and attack even large animals. They possess immense stamina to travel long distances. They use scent markings to claim their territory, communicating: "This territory is occupied. This territory is mine!"

The word *wolf* is also used in reference to people who are:

- Known to be "wolves in sheep's clothing" by cloaking their intentions beneath an innocent, friendly manner.

- Known to be forward, direct, and zealous in the seduction of women.

- Known to "wolf" down food, eating greedily—devouring their food like prey.

The Bible describes the destruction that wolves can cause:

*"Her officials within her are like **wolves** tearing their prey; they shed blood and kill people to make unjust gain."* (Ezekiel 22:27)

2 Snakes/Serpents/Vipers

These are creeping creatures that can also move rapidly. Although many snakes are harmless, they are most often feared for their hissing, rattling, biting, and stinging. They inflict burning pain and cause inflammation where they bite. Considered cunning and subtle, they can also be malicious and deadly poisonous.

The word *serpent* is also used in reference to people who are:

- Known to be dangerous, treacherous persons.

- Known to inject injurious venom into people or groups by poisoning their minds, hearts, or reputation.

- Known to act silently, secretly, and sinuously to inflict injury on others.

The Bible describes the destructive nature of serpents:

*"They make their tongues as sharp as a **serpent's**; the poison of **vipers** is on their lips."* (Psalm 140:3)

3 Hornets

Hornets are any of the larger social wasps which, because they possess biting mouthparts, can bite and sting at the same time. Just one hornet can mobilize an entire nest to sting aggressively. In a swarm, they can drive cattle and horses to madness, and their formidable stings can also kill human beings.

The word *hornet* is also used in reference to people who are:

- Known to be excessively angry—or "mad as a hornet."

- Known to gather others so as to "swarm" a person or place, thus creating havoc or harm with "stings" (for example, accusations, threats, slander, etc.).

- Known to build a "hornet's nest" of angry, venomous people who can be deadly.

The Bible depicts their devastating ability in this description:

*"I sent the **hornet** ahead of you, which drove them out before you—also the two Amorite kings. You did not do it with your own sword and bow."* (Joshua 24:12)

THREE AVOIDERS: Inwardly Passive

1 Tortoises

Tortoises are protected by large, dome-shaped shells that are difficult for predators to crack. They withdraw their necks into their shells by folding them under their spines or folding their necks to the side. Tortoises possess excellent nighttime vision but poor daytime vision because of their color blindness. They have short, sturdy feet famous for moving slowly, partly because of their heavy shells, but also because of their relatively inefficient, sprawling gait.

The word *tortoise* (or turtle) is also used in reference to people who are:

• Known for being slow or for being stragglers.

• Known for "withdrawing into a shell" when threatened.

• Known for dawdling or shirking responsibility.

In the Bible, *"any kind of great lizard"* would include **tortoises** (Leviticus 11:29–30).

2 Chameleons

Chameleons can change to a variety of colors—brown, green, blue, yellow, red, black, or white—in response to temperature, light, and mood. A calm chameleon can be green, but when angry, it can turn yellow. Chameleons possess elongated tongues that can be up to twice the length of their bodies, and their eyes move independently of each other, giving sharp, stereoscopic vision and depth perception.

The word *chameleon* is also used in reference to people who are:

- Known to change their minds or even their characters, but only superficially, merely to be expedient.

- Known for their quick or frequent changes, especially in appearance in order to "fit in."

- Known to blend in with diverse groups by reflecting each group's look, behavior, and belief when with the group.

The Bible states, *"These are unclean for you … the **chameleon**."* (Leviticus 11:29–30)

3 Weasels

Weasels have a reputation for cleverness and guile, especially as they perform a "hypnotic dance" in front of their prey. These small, furry animals can twist and burrow down into small holes. They produce a thick, oily, powerful smelling liquid called musk, used for scent marking and defense.

The word *weasel* is also used in reference to people who are:

- Known to act deviously, unscrupulously, and underhandedly.

- Known to use "weasel words" in order to be evasive or insincere.

- Known to evade or escape from a situation by "weaseling out" of it.

In the Bible, *"the rat"* would include the **weasel** (Leviticus 11:29).

CHARACTERISTICS OF DYSFUNCTIONAL CONFLICT

It was a classic case of sibling rivalry, except that it originated in the womb. Rebekah sensed more than just the random kicking of tiny feet within her, there was a real struggle going on. The Lord explained, *"Two nations are in your womb, and two peoples from within you will be separated; one people will be stronger than the other, and the older will serve the younger."* (Genesis 25:23)

On the day of the twins' birth, Esau arrived first, reddish and covered with hair. Jacob quickly followed, his hand holding his brother's heel, a foretelling image of the position he would usurp from his brother. The name, Jacob, means "He takes by the heel" or "He cheats."

The two brothers could not have been more different. Esau was a masterful hunter, the proverbial outdoorsman, while Jacob was reserved, preferring to remain indoors and cook. Esau was brash and brazen; Jacob was cool and calculating, as evidenced by the red stew incident when Esau, exhausted from a day of working in the field, wanted some of what Jacob had boiling in a pot. His brother obliged him, but only after buying Esau's birthright (Genesis 25:31).

Jacob later deceived his aging father, Isaac, by claiming to be Esau and thereby obtained the sought-after blessing of the firstborn. This deception prompted threats of murder from his brother, Esau.

WHAT ARE Common Statements Used in Conflict?[9]

Conflict—it happens to the best of us. Two of God's premier workers in the early days of the church, Paul and Barnabas, had *"a sharp disagreement"* (Acts 15:39) that resulted in their going their separate ways. The cause for contention was that Barnabas wanted to take his cousin John Mark with him and Paul as they revisited cities where they had ministered.

Paul disagreed, mindful of John Mark's deserting them on a previous mission trip. John Mark had obviously regained the trust of Barnabas, but not of Paul. Their differences were resolved by the launching of two missionary journeys instead of one with Barnabas and his cousin going to Cyprus and with Paul and Silas going to Syria and Cilicia.

> "I appeal to you ... that all of you agree with one another."
> (1 Corinthians 1:10)

Who Are Attackers and Avoiders?

Seven Faulty Accusations of Attackers

- "You'll never change!"
- "You are always against me!"
- "You will reject me—it's just a matter of time!"
- "You can never be trusted!"
- "You've failed too much—you are a failure!"
- "You are hopeless—there's no hope for you!"
- "You are totally at fault if this relationship fails!"

Seven Faulty Expectations of Avoiders

- "You should never create conflict in our relationship."
- "You will always see things my way if you truly love me."
- "You will always do things my way if you are loyal to me."
- "You must never get angry with me because I will not be able to handle it."
- "You must look only to me to meet all of your needs."
- "You are to look only to me to make you happy."
- "You will always need me to make you secure."

Each of us begins to develop a style of handling conflict at an early age. Our personal ways of "fighting" come from our natural instinct, personality, and early family dynamics. Many of us are unable to defuse conflict because we are repeating the extreme patterns of childhood, either *attacking* or *avoiding*. Those in these two different categories can be thought of as either *attackers* or *avoiders*. Considering the characteristics of the six "critters" mentioned earlier will help define the personalities of the two categories. The problem with both of these styles is that neither strategy appropriates the grace that is available to a child of God.[11]

"See to it that no one misses the grace of God and that no bitter root grows up to cause trouble and defile many."
(Hebrews 12:15)

Attackers: Outwardly Aggressive

1 *The Wolf* [12]—alias *Dictator*

(a person granted absolute power, holding complete autocratic control)

- Seeks to control everyone and everything
- Judges the actions and motives of others
- Refuses to listen to opposing opinions with an open mind

- Uses criticism to cut people down
- Engages in power plays

Message: "Give in to me or I'll attack you!"

Goal: To feel powerful

"Watch out for false prophets. They come to you in sheep's clothing, but inwardly they are ferocious wolves." (Matthew 7:15)

2 The Snake[13]—alias *Backbiter*

(a person who says mean or spiteful things behind another person's back)

- Bites when you're not looking
- Uses criticism and "put-downs"
- Starts false rumors
- Pretends to have done nothing wrong
- Gathers allies

Message: "Don't tangle with me or you will regret it later."

Goal: To feel superior

"You brood of vipers, how can you who are evil say anything good? For out of the overflow of the heart the mouth speaks." (Matthew 12:34)

3 The Hornet[14]—alias *Faultfinder*

(a person who is disposed to find fault, is critical, petty, and nagging)

- Registers repetitive complaints
- Makes negative statements about everything

- Blames others
- Pulls others into disagreements
- Delights in misery

Message: "Don't get on my bad side or I'll talk about you!"

Goal: To feel valuable

"A fool's mouth is his undoing, and his lips are a snare to his soul." (Proverbs 18:7)

Avoiders: Inwardly Passive

1 *The Turtle*[15]—alias *Retreater*

(a person who withdraws from what is difficult, dangerous, or disagreeable)

- Plays dumb
- Gives one-word answers
- Withdraws
- Seeks secrecy
- Makes you feel guilty for asking questions

Message: "Don't confront me because it won't do any good."

Goal: To feel safe

"A truthful witness saves lives, but a false witness is deceitful." (Proverbs 14:25)

2 *The Chameleon*[16]—alias *Obliger*

(a person who is bound in some way to another or is in someone's debt for a favor or service)

- Avoids making decisions
- Acts innocent
- Appears nice and agreeable
- Recoils from making a commitment
- Downplays differences

Message: "I'm nice to you; you owe it to me to be nice back."

Goal: To feel accepted

"Fear of man will prove to be a snare."
(Proverbs 29:25)

3 *The Weasel*[17]—alias *Twister*

(a person who perverts meanings, squirms, is devious, and uses gimmicks)

- Uses clever defensives
- Sidesteps the issue
- Twists and bends the truth
- Blames others
- Avoids "I" statements

Message: "I'm not going to get pinned down."

Goal: To feel confident

"A man of perverse heart does not prosper; he whose tongue is deceitful falls into trouble."
(Proverbs 17:20)

Who Displays Which Style of Conflict in Scripture?

Based on the thousands of narratives throughout the Bible, even the novice reader sees that negative conflict has been "alive and well" from the beginning of time. For example, Abraham, on two different occasions, lies about his relationship with Sarah, his wife—he passes her off as his sister. Because of her beauty, he fears that both monarchs will kill him in order to take her. Because of his fear, Abraham acts like a turtle, hiding in its shell.

A different kind of avoider is Abraham's grandson Jacob. He wants the birthright due his older twin brother. Instead of telling the truth, deceitful Jacob lies, connives, and weasels his way into his father's presence and blessing. Jacob is a weasel of the first order!

Which type of attacker or avoider is each of the following people? (At times, a person may not be in conflict, but then later a major conflict flames.) Analyze and identify the negative conflict styles in each of the following relationships. (Hint: Read the Scripture first. Then fill in the blanks. The first two are done for you.)

Relationship #1: Between the Serpent, Adam, and Eve

The Serpent: _He is an attacker, a snake. He plays the part of himself!_

"The serpent was more crafty than any of the wild animals the LORD God had made. He said to the woman [Eve], 'Did God really say, "You must not eat from any tree in the garden"?'" (Genesis 3:1)

Adam: _He is an avoider, a weasel. He tried to weasel out of accepting responsibility for his wrong choices by blaming Eve!_

"The man [Adam] said, 'The woman you put here with me—she gave me some fruit from the tree, and I ate it.'" (Genesis 3:12)

Eve: _____

_____

"Then the LORD God said to the woman [Eve], 'What is this you have done?' The woman said, 'The serpent deceived me, and I ate.'" (Genesis 3:13)

Relationship #2: Cain toward Abel

Cain: _____

_____

"Cain said to his brother Abel, 'Let's go out to the field.' And while they were in the field, Cain attacked his brother Abel and killed him." (Genesis 4:8)

Relationship #3: Between the Philistines, Delilah, and Samson

The Philistines: _____

_____

"The rulers of the Philistines went to her and said, 'See if you can lure him into showing you the secret of his great strength and how we can overpower him so we may tie him up and subdue him. Each one of us will give you eleven hundred shekels of silver.'" (Judges 16:5)

Delilah: _____

_____

"She said to him, 'How can you say, "I love you," when you won't confide in me? This is the third time you have made a fool of me and haven't told me the secret of your great strength.' With such nagging she prodded him day after day until he was tired to death." (Judges 16:15–16)

Samson: _____

_____

"So he told her everything. 'No razor has ever been used on my head,' he said, 'because I have been a Nazirite set apart to God since birth. If my head were shaved, my strength would leave me, and I would become as weak as any other man.'" (Judges 16:17)

King Saul toward David

King Saul: _____

_____

"He [Saul] raved within his house while David was playing the lyre, as he did day by day. Saul had his spear in his hand. And Saul hurled the spear, for he thought, 'I will pin David to the wall.' But David evaded him twice." (1 Samuel 18:10–11 ESV)

King David toward Bathsheba

King David: _____

_____

"This is what the LORD, the God of Israel, says … 'Why did you despise the word of the LORD by doing what is evil in his eyes? You struck down Uriah the Hittite with the sword and took his wife to be your own. You killed him with the sword of the Ammonites. Now, therefore, the sword will never depart from your house, because you despised me and took the wife of Uriah the Hittite to be your own.'" (2 Samuel 12:7, 9–10)

Relationship #6: **The Pharisees toward Jesus**

Pharisees: _____

_____

*"Jesus said to the crowds and to his disciples ...
'Woe to you, teachers of the law and Pharisees,
you hypocrites! You shut the kingdom of heaven
in men's faces. You yourselves do not enter,
nor will you let those enter who are trying
to. ... You snakes! You brood of vipers! How
will you escape being condemned to hell?'"*
(Matthew 23:1, 13, 33)

Relationship #7: **Pilate toward Jesus**

Pilate: _____

_____

*"On hearing this, Pilate asked if the man was a
Galilean. When he learned that Jesus was under
Herod's jurisdiction, he sent him to Herod, who
was also in Jerusalem at that time."* (Luke 23:6–7)

Relationship #8: **Judas toward Jesus**

Judas: _____

_____

*"Judas Iscariot ... asked, 'What are you willing
to give me if I hand him over to you?' So
they counted out for him thirty silver coins."*
(Matthew 26:14–15)

Relationship #9: Martha toward Jesus

Martha: _____

_____

"Martha was distracted by all the preparations that had to be made. She came to him and asked, 'Lord, don't you care that my sister has left me to do the work by myself? Tell her to help me!'" (Luke 10:40)

Relationship #10: Peter toward Jesus

Peter: _____

_____

"Peter was sitting out in the courtyard, and a servant girl came to him. 'You also were with Jesus of Galilee,' she said. But he denied it before them all. 'I don't know what you're talking about,' he said. Then he went out to the gateway, where another girl saw him and said to the people there, 'This fellow was with Jesus of Nazareth.' He denied it again, with an oath: 'I don't know the man!' After a little while, those standing there went up to Peter and said, 'Surely you are one of them, for your accent gives you away.' Then he began to call down curses on himself and he swore to them, 'I don't know the man!' Immediately a rooster crowed." (Matthew 26:69–74)

(Note: If you are still stumped, the answers can be found on page 89.)

CAUSES OF CONFLICT

Mix two or more people together and you have a montage of differing personalities, priorities, perceptions, and preferences—a concoction ripe for *conflict*. Often the result is fingers pointed in accusation rather than hands shaking in agreement. Random words of blessing can be quickly eaten up by words of bitterness.

Conflict was experienced by the first family God created, conflict among Adam and Eve and their offspring, and it is still being experienced in homes today, as well as in workplaces and churches and among nations. Who hasn't at times wanted to throw their hands up in the air and exclaim, "Why can't we all just get along?" *Well, we can*—with the empowerment of God and through our obedience to Him. His Word provides principles for peace that can bring about the supernatural result of reconciliation and resolution, from the board room to the bedroom.

"Encourage one another and build each other up, just as in fact you are doing."
(1 Thessalonians 5:11)

Everyone has it … no one wants it … no one can escape it! What is *it*? One common denominator for us all is *conflict*. But where does it come from? People are who they are and act the way they act as a result of a combination of factors.

Natural temperament or personality types

▶ You were born with a natural bent toward being outgoing or reserved, compliant or defiant, aggressive or passive.

▶ Your temperament/personality traits can work to your advantage or disadvantage depending on whether you learn to use them productively in resolving conflicts or destructively in creating conflicts.

"Not that we are competent in ourselves to claim anything for ourselves, but our competence comes from God." (2 Corinthians 3:5)

Early childhood experiences

▶ You were deeply influenced by your early family relationships through words you heard and behaviors you saw that gave you messages about "who you are" and "what you do" and how to respond to conflict.

▶ You can change the assumptions you adopted about yourself and about conflict resolution that are influencing your behavior today by identifying the messages you received growing up in your family and evaluating them as to whether they are helpful or harmful.

"Let us discern for ourselves what is right; let us learn together what is good." (Job 34:4)

Physical factors

▶ You were born with certain physical characteristics such as brain chemistry that may be affecting the way you respond to the rush of adrenaline experienced during times of conflict.

▶ You can have a thorough medical check-up. When experiencing a conflict, you may even want to have an evaluation about brain chemistry. Did you know that you can learn ways to actually change the chemistry of your brain if it is causing you problems in conflict resolution?

"He sent forth his word and healed them; he rescued them from the grave." (Psalm 107:20)

Learned behaviors

▶ You may have *unintentionally* learned patterns of responding to conflict by following the example of significant people in your life and may be subconsciously modeling your behavior after those who either attack or avoid conflict.

▶ You can *intentionally* unlearn a behavior pattern by determining to learn new behaviors and by modeling yourself after people who embrace conflicts as a fact of life and who find ways of productively resolving them.

"Let the wise listen and add to their learning, and let the discerning get guidance." (Proverbs 1:5)

We are all created with three God-given inner needs—the need for love, significance, and security.[18] These needs can be translated into the need to feel heard and understood, to feel encouraged and at peace, to feel affirmed and accepted, to feel confident and courageous. Or these needs can be negatively translated into the need to feel superior. Unmet needs can become the driving force behind why we act the way we act when we are faced with a conflict. The challenge, of course, is to find a way to get our legitimate needs met legitimately rather than illegitimately, and that can be accomplished only through a personal, intimate relationship with Jesus Christ.

> "His divine power has given us everything we need for life and godliness through our knowledge of him who called us by his own glory and goodness."
> (2 Peter 1:3)

Attackers Feel Insignificant

▶ *Wolves* have a goal to feel *powerful*.

Children who grow up feeling insignificant within their families typically become driven by the need to feel significant. This drive can result in finding destructive ways of meeting this need.

Children who feel powerless can develop aggressive tactics to overpower others. These newly developed *wolves* become fiercely competitive in order to feel like true "winners." They become dictatorial in order to feel powerful. Thus, their need to feel significant is met temporarily.

▶ ***Serpents*** have a goal to feel *superior*.

Children who grow up regularly experiencing "put-downs" and are the target of belittling comments may become driven by the need to overcome feelings of inferiority.

Children who feel inferior can become behind-the-scene backbiters. These newly developed serpents spread poisonous rumors in order to feel superior to others temporarily.

▶ ***Hornets*** have a goal to feel *valuable*.

Children who grow up being told that "children are to be seen but not heard" or whose opinions and feelings are virtually discounted typically may become driven by the need to be valuable, to be heard and understood.

Children who don't feel valuable typically can develop a negative attitude. Making constant complaints is a way to get the ear of others, leaving these newly developed hornets feeling valuable enough to be heard and understood temporarily.

Avoiders Feel Insecure

▶ *Tortoises* have a goal to feel *safe*.

Children who grow up in homes where anger is unrestrained and conflict goes unresolved and where little positive occurs typically become driven by the need for peace.

Children who don't feel "safe" typically make being safe their life goal, seeking to protect themselves from "danger." By turning inward and emotionally walling themselves off from others, these newly developed tortoises feel a sense of safety temporarily.

▶ *Chameleons* have a goal to feel *accepted*.

Children who grow up with criticism and negative feedback from significant adults in their lives and who don't receive compliments and praise typically become driven by the need for acceptance.

Children starved for acceptance can become classic people-pleasers. They do whatever they think is necessary in order to make and keep everyone happy so as not to be criticized or rejected, leaving them—these newly developed chameleons—feeling accepted temporarily.

▶ **Weasels** have a goal to feel *confident*.

Children who grow up with an overprotective, controlling parent—and who have no firm boundaries or personal accountability for their actions—typically become driven by the need for confidence.

Children who lack courage to take a stand find that becoming shrewd and evasive rather than honest and forthright keeps them "out of trouble." This leaves these newly developed *weasels* with a sense of *confidence* and *courage* temporarily.

"My God will meet all your needs according to his glorious riches in Christ Jesus."
(Philippians 4:19)

Conflict with people is one matter—but conflict with God is another. Why is conflict with God the *worst* conflict? Can you imagine the small parts of a watch refusing to operate as the watchmaker designed them to operate? What if the hands of a watch moved in the opposite direction? The watch would be useless. You're not useless, but you're a lot like that watch. When God created you, He had a plan for you. But when you refuse to yield your will to Him, you miss His plan and purpose for your life. This means you are in conflict with Him—the very One who loves you and created you. God wants a relationship with you. Then He will fulfill the very purpose for which you were created. The Lord says,

"I know the plans I have for you ...
plans to prosper you and not to harm you,
plans to give you hope and a future."
(Jeremiah 29:11)

How to Resolve Your Conflict with God

There are *four* spiritual truths you need to know.

1 Your Problem—*You (like everyone else) have chosen to sin.*

We all have *chosen* wrong, we all have sinned—not one of us is perfect. Each time we choose to go our own way, not God's way, we are in conflict with Him. The Bible says that we "sin."

"We all, like sheep, have gone astray, each of us has turned to his own way." (Isaiah 53:6)

2 Your Position—*Your sin separates you from God.*

Because God is without sin (God's character is perfect), our sin puts us in conflict with God. This spiritual conflict results in a *penalty* or a *consequence.* The Bible says that the consequence of our sin is to be separated from God's presence. This separation is called *spiritual death.*

"Your iniquities have separated you from your God . ... The wages of sin is death, but the gift of God is eternal life in Christ Jesus our Lord." (Isaiah 59:2; Romans 6:23)

3 Your Provision—*God provided the way for you to be relieved from the consequence of spiritual death.*

Sin is serious because it separates us from God. Because God is just, He cannot ignore our wrongdoing. But because of His love, He doesn't want us separated from Him. This creates a dilemma. He has to punish sin, yet He does not want us to die and be permanently separated from Him. This is why the heavenly Father sent His own Son, Jesus, to come to earth for the purpose of dying on the cross for our sins—Jesus actually *chose* to pay the penalty for our sins. We should have died, but instead, Christ died for us.

"God demonstrates his own love for us in this: While we were still sinners, Christ died for us." (Romans 5:8)

4 Your Part—*You can move from spiritual death to spiritual life now, and experience His peace.*

We must seek God's forgiveness God's way. You need to trust that Jesus Christ died as your substitute and ask Him to come into your life to take control of your life. This is God's only acceptable plan. Jesus said,

"I am the way and the truth and the life. No one comes to the Father except through me." (John 14:6)

By believing in (relying on) Jesus alone to pay the penalty for your sins and yielding your will to His will, you are truly forgiven of your sins. And when you are forgiven, you are not only cleansed from all of your sin (past, present, and future), but you also have peace with God—saved from staying in conflict with God. The Bible says,

"God so loved the world that he gave his one and only Son, that whoever believes in him shall not perish but have eternal life. For God did not send his Son into the world to condemn the world, but to save the world through him." (John 3:16–17)

If you desire to have peace with God—so that you will not be in conflict with Him any longer, you can tell Him in a simple, heartfelt prayer like this:

MY PRAYER FOR PEACE WITH GOD

"Lord Jesus, I need You.
I admit that I have sinned.
I understand that the punishment for my
sin is death and to be spiritually separated
from You. Yet, because of Your love, Your
plan is to save me. I believe that what
You said in Your Word is true—that You
sent Jesus Christ to pay the penalty that I
should have to pay. Jesus, thank You for
dying on the cross for my sins and taking
the punishment in my place.
Right now I ask You to come into my life to
be my Lord and Savior.
Take control of my life and make me the
person You created me to be.
Thank You for Your unconditional love.
And thank You for Your peace.
In Your holy name. Amen."

If you sincerely prayed this prayer, listen to what God says:

"The peace of God, which transcends all understanding, will guard your hearts and your minds in Christ Jesus."
(Philippians 4:7)

49

Conflict came hurling at Paul that day, one stone at a time.

His Jewish brethren, proponents of legalism and opponents of the gospel of grace, spurred a crowd to throw stones at Paul—a crowd that only moments before had sought to offer sacrifices to him as to a god for his healing of a crippled man. After the stoning, Paul was dragged out of their city and left for dead. However, when his disciples gathered around him, he got up and went into the city of Lystra and on to Derbe with Barnabas the next day.

As they traveled, Paul and Barnabas, recognizing that opposition and conflict are inevitable, encouraged the followers of Jesus they encountered, *"encouraging them to remain true to the faith. 'We must go through many hardships to enter the kingdom of God,' they said"* (Acts 14:22).

The reason we all experience conflict is rooted in a system of wrong beliefs. We assume that what we want is what we need and that it is up to us to defeat those who oppose us. After all, if we don't protect our interests, who will? This fear-based thinking causes us to selfishly respond by either attacking or avoiding people or situations we perceive to be threatening.[19]

▶ WRONG BELIEF

"I am afraid of conflict because it reflects negatively on me. To feel secure and significant, I must get rid of conflict by either conquering it, compromising it, or avoiding it."

▶ RIGHT BELIEF

"I know that conflict is a natural result of living with different types of people. My sense of security and significance is based on my identity in Christ and in His perfect love and acceptance of me."

> "There is no fear in love. But perfect love drives out fear, because fear has to do with punishment. The one who fears is not made perfect in love."
> (1 John 4:18)

STEPS TO SOLUTION

God honored the request of this twenty-year-old —and then some:

> "Give your servant a discerning heart to govern your people and to distinguish between right and wrong. For who is able to govern this great people of yours?"
> (1 Kings 3:9)

Solomon knew that God's kindness to his father, David, was a result of his father's faithfulness to God evidenced by righteous attitudes and actions. Now that Solomon is king, he feels the heavy weight of being the leader and judge of God's people. Therefore, he confesses his own inadequacies, considering himself a mere child before God, and acknowledges his dependence on God for wisdom in resolving the conflicts of his people.

It so pleased the Lord that Solomon had asked for a wise and discerning mind that He not only gave him wisdom like no other but also bestowed riches and honor on him as well as the promise of a long life if he obeyed the Lord.

Solomon soon needed to call on that wisdom:

"Two prostitutes came to the king and stood before him. One of them said, 'My lord, this woman and I live in the same house. I had a baby while she was there with me. The third day after my child

was born, this woman also had a baby. We were alone; there was no one in the house but the two of us. During the night this woman's son died because she lay on him. So she got up in the middle of the night and took my son from my side while I your servant was asleep. She put him by her breast and put her dead son by my breast. ...' The other woman said, 'No! The living one is my son; the dead one is yours.' But the first one insisted, 'No! The dead one is yours. ...' And so they argued before the king." (1 Kings 3:16–22)

KEY VERSE TO MEMORIZE

"Let us therefore make every effort to do what leads to peace and to mutual edification." (Romans 14:19)

Seven Principles for Facing Conflict

Book of Philemon verses 1–25

1. **HUMILITY**—Don't use your higher position to take advantage of those in a lower position.

   "Therefore, although in Christ I could be bold and order you to do what you ought to do, yet I prefer to appeal to you on the basis of love. It is as none other than Paul—an old man and now also a prisoner of Christ Jesus..." (vv. 8–9)

2. **INTEGRITY**—Be absolutely honest about the problems.

"...that I appeal to you for my son Onesimus, who became my son while I was in chains. Formerly he was useless to you, but now he has become useful both to you and to me." (vv. 10–11)

3. **VULNERABILITY**—Share your heart feelings.

"I am sending him—who is my very heart—back to you. I would have liked to keep him with me so that he could take your place in helping me while I am in chains for the gospel." (vv. 12–13)

4. **SUBMISSION**—Don't force an action not under your control.

"But I did not want to do anything without your consent..." (v. 14a)

5. **OPTIMISM**—Expect the best of another.

"... so that any favor you do would not seem forced but would be voluntary." (v. 14b)

6. **FAITH**—Remember the sovereign hand of God.[20]

"Perhaps the reason he was separated from you for a little while was that you might have him back forever—no longer as a slave, but better than a slave, as a dear brother. He is very dear to me but even dearer to you, both as a fellow man and as a brother in the Lord." (vv. 15–16)

7. **EXHORTATION**—Choose your words carefully.

"Confident of your obedience, I write to you, knowing that you will do even more than I ask." (v. 21)

How to Apply the Five *W*'s and an *H* to Conflict Resolution

Who? Who is involved in the conflict?
- Name those presently involved in the conflict.
- List those who could be involved to bring about a solution.

What? What is your goal?
- Put into writing what you want done.
- Be clear—is this a one-time goal or a long-term goal?

Why? Why do you want to do it?
- List the reasons for taking action.
- List what will happen if you do not take action.

Where? Where will it happen?
- Assess where you assume the conflict could be resolved.
- Evaluate whether it could happen at another place.

When? When do you want it done?
- Establish a timeline from beginning to end.
- List short-term, measurable goals.

How? How do you want it done?
- List the policies and procedures that need to be put in place.
- List the guidelines needed to accomplish the goal.

"Plans fail for lack of counsel,
but with many advisers they succeed."
(Proverbs 15:22)

Human nature says respond "in kind" to others—insult for insult, blow for blow. One of the clearest challenges of Christ is to not respond "in kind," but to respond "in the Spirit." To be Spirit-controlled rather than situation-controlled is not **natural** to human nature. Being Spirit-controlled **becomes natural** to the new nature that a believer receives at salvation—the very nature and mind of Christ. Undoubtedly, to counter evil for evil is natural, but to counter evil with good is the supernatural work of Christ within you.

> "Do not be overcome by evil,
> but overcome evil with good."
> (Romans 12:21)

▶ **Be discerning** regarding the accuracy of the critical words of others.

Pray: "Lord, help me not to accept all critical words as true, nor to reject all words as lies. Enable me to discern the false from the true. Put a hedge of protection around my mind so that I reject the lies. Allow my heart to accept constructive criticism that You may bring freedom to my life and change me."

"The wise in heart are called discerning, and pleasant words promote instruction." (Proverbs 16:21)

▶ **Be open** to the slightest kernel of truth when you are criticized.

Pray: "Lord, if there is any truth in the critical words said about me, please convict my heart so that I might confess it and cooperate with You to change it."

"A rebuke impresses a man of discernment more than a hundred lashes a fool." (Proverbs 17:10)

▶ **Be willing** to consider the criticism. If it is true, this person is God's megaphone to get your attention.

Pray: "Lord, I accept this criticism as Your way of teaching me something I need to know. Please reveal to me what it is You are saying to me through the criticism."

"The way of a fool seems right to him, but a wise man listens to advice." (Proverbs 12:15)

▶ **Be able** to receive criticism without being defensive.[21]

• Admit to any truth in the criticism.

• Agree when you are in error.

• Ask for further correction.

Pray: "Lord, I admit that I (state the offense). I agree that I was wrong. Please continue to use others to put me on a correction course when I'm off track in my attitudes or actions. And please continue to transform me more and more into the character of Christ."

"A mocker resents correction; he will not consult the wise." (Proverbs 15:12)

▶ **Be determined** to speak well of your critic.

Pray: "Lord, I yield my tongue to You. I ask that You place a guard over my mouth so that I will only speak the truth in love to (name) and will always speak well of (name) to others. I pledge to focus on the good in (name) and not on the bad."

"Bless those who persecute you; bless and do not curse." (Romans 12:14)

▶ **Be dependent** on the Lord's perspective to determine your worth and value, not on the opinions of others.

Pray: "Lord, thank You for establishing my worth and value by dying for me and adopting me into Your family. I will not live for the approval of people because I have Your approval, and that is all I need. Thank You for loving me."

"Am I now trying to win the approval of men, or of God? Or am I trying to please men? If I were still trying to please men, I would not be a servant of Christ." (Galatians 1:10)

Boundaries are *established limits*—lines not to be crossed. When a boundary is exceeded, the result is a repercussion. If a boundary is honored, the result is a reward. When parents establish boundaries, their children are the ones who choose to go beyond the boundaries or to stay within them. This means that the children, not the parents, are the ones who choose the repercussion or the *reward*. The same is true when adults establish boundaries with one another as peers, friends, or spouses. This principle is clearly demonstrated when God set a *boundary* with Adam and Eve. In choosing to go beyond the boundary God established for them, they *chose* the consequence of their sin—they *chose* the repercussion.

> **"To Adam he said, 'Because you listened to your wife and ate from the tree about which I commanded you, "You must not eat of it," Cursed is the ground because of you; through painful toil you will eat of it all the days of your life.'"** (Genesis 3:17)

▶ Boundaries are …

- The limits that establish a border (like a curb).
- The realization that we are separate from one another.
- The basis of our individual identity.

▶ Boundaries say …

- What we are and what we are not.
- What we will choose and what we will not choose.
- What we will endure and what we will not endure.
- What we feel and what we do not feel.
- What we like and what we do not like.
- What we want and what we do not want.

▶ Boundaries help …

Jesus pronounced, *"I did not come to bring peace, but a sword"* (Matthew 10:34). Jesus clearly communicated that we must seek to resolve what is wrong by cutting to the heart of the matter. He announced that *"the truth will set you free"* (John 8:32). At certain times, the sword of truth is necessary in order to live a life of integrity and make needed changes. When you do what is right in His sight, Jesus will give you His supernatural peace. Although not everything around you is peaceful, He can give you an internal *"peace that transcends all understanding."* (Philippians 4:7)

Establishing Boundaries

▶ ***Do*** Communicate your expectations clearly.

- Get on the person's eye level.
- Prior to any problems, describe in detail what you expect of the person regarding your relationship.

- Form an agreement and ask for a statement of the person's understanding of your expectations.

- When it is time for compliance with your agreement, give a gentle reminder.

Example of *Parent to Child*

Don't Say: "Don't you think it is time for you to go to bed now?"

Do Say: "Remember, we agreed that your bedtime is 8:30. It is 8:20; so what do you need to be doing now?"

Example of *Adult to Adult*

Don't Say: "It is time for you to come home so we won't be late for dinner."

Do Say: "I'm just calling to let you know I will be ready to serve dinner at six o'clock as we have agreed. If you aren't home by 6:20 or do not call, the children and I will go ahead and eat so they can start their homework."

> "Simply let your 'Yes' be 'Yes,'
> and your 'No,' 'No.'"
> (Matthew 5:37)

▶ *Do* Establish negative repercussions for breaking an agreement.

- To establish effective repercussions, know what will make an impact.

- If possible, choose a repercussion related to the offensive behavior.

- Clearly communicate the repercussion.

- Prior to a problem, get the person's agreement to the repercussion.
- Allow the person to experience the repercussion if the agreement is broken.

Example of *Parent to Child*

Tommy, age ten, lives on a busy street. He likes to ride his bicycle with his friend who lives across the street, but he was told never to cross the street without an adult. If Tommy disobeys, the *repercussion* is that he will not be allowed to ride his bicycle the next day.

Example of *Adult to Adult*

Joe and Jennifer agree that he will leave work in time to pick her up at home at six o'clock and they will join some friends for dinner at a restaurant across town. The agreement is that Joe will be sure to pick Jennifer up on time since they have reservations and can't be late. If Joe breaks their agreement by being late, the *repercussion* is that Jennifer will go to the restaurant without him even though Joe does not like for them to go places separately.

"No discipline seems pleasant at the time, but painful. Later on, however, it produces a harvest of righteousness and peace for those who have been trained by it."
(Hebrews 12:11)

When life hands you lemons, make lemonade! If you add the right ingredients, the same transformation may occur in your communication with a loved one. Practice following this easy recipe, and taste the sweetness of resolving painful differences.

> **"Pleasant words are a honeycomb, sweet to the soul and healing to the bones." (Proverbs 16:24)**

CONFRONT

The struggler squeezes all the juice out of the lemon. Plan a time to meet with your offender in order to release the juice from your lemon.

When one of you feels sour (hurt, frustrated, or unjustly treated), don't hold it in.

COMMUNICATE FEELINGS

Express your anger or unmet need by squeezing out the truth in a loving, non-accusatory way.

▶ Share the problem using "I" statements.

"I'm feeling betrayed. Would you be willing to listen?"

▶ Describe only the upsetting words or behavior without criticizing character.

▶ Do not accuse, belittle, call names, or criticize.

"Reckless words pierce like a sword, but the tongue of the wise brings healing." (Proverbs 12:18)

"The tongue of the righteous is choice silver … The lips of the righteous nourish many, but fools die for lack of judgment." (Proverbs 10:20–21)

▶ Instead, notice what Paul wrote:

"Speaking the truth in love, we will in all things grow up into him who is the Head, that is, Christ. … 'In your anger do not sin': Do not let the sun go down while you are still angry." (Ephesians 4:15, 26)

COMPLY

The listener is a pitcher receiving *all* the juice.

The person being confronted indicates a **willingness to listen** (to receive the rebuke without becoming angry or defensive) and sincerely seeks to hear the speaker's pain.

▶ Respond with a willingness to give undivided attention.

▶ Do not interrupt. Hear the problem to the "last drop."

▶ Above all, don't make excuses or become defensive.

"Submit to one another out of reverence for Christ." (Ephesians 5:21)

CONFIRM

The listener fills the pitcher with water with no acidic words.

The listener now **paraphrases the problem back** (repeats what is heard) without reacting negatively.

▶ Affirm what is being said.

"You are saying that you felt betrayed last night when I did not defend you? Is this correct?"

▶ Agreement with the facts is not necessary; therefore, do not attempt to justify anything.

▶ Ask if your restating of the problem is correct. If it is not, seek to understand what was said and repeat all.

"He who listens to a life-giving rebuke will be at home among the wise." (Proverbs 15:31)

CHANGE

The struggler asks for sugar. If the receiver gives the sugar, the entire flavor changes!

After feelings have been delivered and received, the struggler is allowed to ***request a change in behavior***. Willingness to listen and change behavior becomes the sweet ingredient for developing intimacy in the relationship.

▶ The struggler makes a request.

"When someone criticizes me in front of you, would you be willing to express emotional support by making a comment on my behalf or by walking away or asking the person to not talk about me when I'm not present to respond?"

▶ Listener identifies some acceptable responses for use in the future.

▶ Listener is willing to please the other with a commitment to change.

"Each of you should look not only to your own interests, but also to the interests of others." (Philippians 2:4)

COMFORT

The listener mixes the sugar and lemon juice well so there is no hint of the sour lemon. After a change in behavior has been agreed on, the listener expresses sorrow over the struggler's pain and expresses appreciation for the opportunity to resolve the problem.

▶ Address the struggler's pain.

"I am so sorry my actions hurt your feelings and caused you to feel betrayed."

▶ Applaud the struggler for approaching you.

▶ Appreciate being given a chance to change your behavior in the future in order to improve your relationship.

"A word aptly spoken is like apples of gold in settings of silver." (Proverbs 25:11)

The dispute presented to Solomon concerns two baby boys, one dead and one alive, and the conflicting testimonies of their prostitute mothers (1 Kings 3:22).

How is Solomon to know who is telling the truth and who is lying? There are no witnesses to testify. There is no evidence to introduce. There is no one to identify the baby boys. There is no way to know which baby belongs to which mother. The situation seems impossible to resolve as each mother continues to adamantly claim the living baby as her own.

The wisdom and discernment for which the king prayed is clearly being put to the test, and the resolution he introduces involves the living infant and a sword.

"The king said, 'This one says,
"My son is alive and your son is dead,"
while that one says,
"No! Your son is dead and mine is alive."'
Then the king said, 'Bring me a sword.'
So they brought a sword for the king."
(1 Kings 3:23–24)

Attackers Want to Feel Significant

▶ *Wolves*[22]—Goal: *To feel powerful*

- Let them have their say without interrupting.
- Get their attention with praise.
- Hold your ground. (Match strength with strength.)
- Avoid arguments.
- Don't put yourself down.

"Don't have anything to do with foolish and stupid arguments, because you know they produce quarrels." (2 Timothy 2:23)

▶ *Snakes*[23]—Goal: *To feel superior*

- Be aware of their power to destroy.
- Catch them in a lie.
- Enlist someone to help you confront them in private.
- Expect them to deny what they have done.
- Don't let them get away with an attack.

"If your brother sins against you, go and show him his fault, just between the two of you. If he listens to you, you have won your brother over. But if he will not listen, take one or two others along, so that 'every matter may be established by the testimony of two or three witnesses.' If he refuses to listen to them, tell it to the church; and if he refuses to listen even to the church, treat him as you would a pagan or a tax collector." (Matthew 18:15–17)

▶ *Hornets*[24]—**Goal:** *To feel valuable*

- Learn to cut off negative conversation.
- Respond only to what is important.
- Confront their game-playing.
- Encourage a look at solutions.
- Don't reinforce their complaints.

"Do not let any unwholesome talk come out of your mouths, but only what is helpful for building others up according to their needs, that it may benefit those who listen." (Ephesians 4:29)

Avoiders Want to Feel Secure

▶ *Turtles*[25]—**Goal:** *To feel safe*

- Ask questions that can't be answered with yes or no.
- Seek to get them to talk on the feeling level.
- Hang in there until you get a response.
- Be positive, not critical with them.
- Don't answer for them.

"A man is praised according to his wisdom, but men with warped minds are despised." (Proverbs 12:8)

▶ *Chameleons*[26]—**Goal:** *To feel accepted*

- Make it "okay" to disagree.
- Help them identify priorities.
- Learn their hidden fears.
- Reinforce their decisions.

- Don't accept their "yes" as complete agreement.

"An anxious heart weighs a man down, but a kind word cheers him up." (Proverbs 12:25)

▶ *Weasels—Goal: To feel courage*

- Avoid accusations.
- Don't get drawn into arguments.
- Be strong and immovable.
- Be forgiving.
- Be consistently encouraging.

"As servants of God we commend ourselves in every way: in great endurance; in troubles, hardships and distresses ... in truthful speech and in the power of God; with weapons of righteousness in the right hand and in the left." (2 Corinthians 6:4, 7)

Some resolutions to conflict are not quickly or easily found but require supernatural discernment and wisdom, as in the case of the two prostitutes who came before King Solomon.

Two women are claiming to be the mother of the same child. How does the king determine the truth? This is the dilemma before the king. The truth is needed in order to settle the conflict. In an attempt to get to the truth, Solomon calls for a sword. He will render a fair resolution. The baby is to be cut in half and equally divided between the two women.

The king's strategy works, the true mother cries out that the baby not be killed but be given to the other woman. Conversely, the other woman agrees with the king's fair resolution that neither would have the living child. Thus the truth is revealed and the king's verdict is that the baby be given to his mother, the woman who was willing to give him up in order to save his life.

"He then gave an order: 'Cut the living child in two and give half to one and half to the other.' The woman whose son was alive was filled with compassion for her son and said to the king, 'Please, my lord, give her the living baby! Don't kill him!' But the other said, 'Neither I nor you shall have him. Cut him in two!' Then the king gave his ruling: 'Give the living baby to the first woman. Do not kill him; she is his mother.'" (1 Kings 3:25–27)

As you prepare to walk the road to resolution of a conflict,[27] remember to …

▶ **Pledge** your commitment.

- "I am committed to this relationship."
- "I am committed to reconciliation, if at all possible."

"If it is possible, as far as it depends on you, live at peace with everyone." (Romans 12:18)

▶ **Pray** for yourself.

- "Am I seeing the true issue?"
- "Reveal any personal error I need to face."
- "Prepare the heart of (name) to be open."

"Search me, O God, and know my heart; test me and know my anxious thoughts. See if there is any offensive way in me, and lead me in the way everlasting." (Psalm 139:23–24)

▶ **Prepare** before you ask for a meeting.

- Discern the root cause of the conflict.
- Examine your expectations.
- Decide on positive solutions.
- Use the "Sandwich Technique."

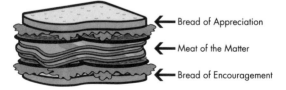

← Bread of Appreciation

← Meat of the Matter

← Bread of Encouragement

"Let us examine our ways and test them, and let us return to the Lord." (Lamentations 3:40)

▶ **Propose** a time to talk face-to-face.

- "I care about our relationship. Is it possible for us to have some time to talk?"
- "I feel there are some unresolved issues that need to be dealt with positively."

"Make every effort to keep the unity of the Spirit through the bond of peace." (Ephesians 4:3)

▶ **Provide** a private place.

- Away from people
- Away from distractions

"If your brother sins against you, go and show him his fault, just between the two of you. If he listens to you, you have won your brother over." (Matthew 18:15)

▶ **Purpose** to be honest. [28]

- Take responsibility for your actions.
- See the other person's viewpoint.

"A truthful witness gives honest testimony, but a false witness tells lies." (Proverbs 12:17)

▶ **Permit** total forgiveness.

- Choose to forgive any hurts.
- Don't mentally rehearse the faults of the other.
- Allow God to reestablish a bond of love.

"Bear with each other and forgive whatever grievances you may have against one another. Forgive as the Lord forgave you. And over all these virtues put on love, which binds them all together in perfect unity." (Colossians 3:13–14)

▶ **Perceive** a future harvest.

- You are sowing seeds that may not take root until later.
- Change is a process.
- What you sow, you reap!

"Let us not become weary in doing good, for at the proper time we will reap a harvest if we do not give up." (Galatians 6:9)

▶ **Present** the present conflict.

- Don't bring up the past.
- Keep the conversation on the present conflict.

"[Love] … does not take into account a wrong suffered." (1 Corinthians 13:5 NASB)

▶ **Promote** fairness and objectivity.

- Avoid generalizations.
- Mention both positives and negatives.

"Do not pervert justice; do not show partiality to the poor or favoritism to the great, but judge your neighbor fairly." (Leviticus 19:15)

▶ **Protect** one another's privacy.

- Don't involve outsiders.
- Control your tongue when you are with other people.

"A gossip betrays a confidence, but a trustworthy man keeps a secret." (Proverbs 11:13)

▶ **Preserve** individuality.

- Value differences in goals, desires, and priorities.
- Don't demand like thinking.

"I too will have my say; I too will tell what I know." (Job 32:17)

▶ **Project** openness and optimism.

- Exhibit positive body language.
- Use "I" statements and make good eye contact.

"Encourage one another and build each other up, just as in fact you are doing." (1 Thessalonians 5:11)

▶ **Practice** love.

- End with an appropriate physical expression: firm handshake, hug, or a pat on the back.
- Express appreciation, care, and love.

"A friend loves at all times, and a brother is born for adversity." (Proverbs 17:17)

Forgiveness is not contingent on resolution, nor is it based on feelings. Forgiveness is a choice—a choice to do what God tells you to do. Realize that when Jesus was being crucified on the cross, He said,

> "Father, forgive them, for they do not know what they are doing." (Luke 23:34)

He knew they hadn't changed. If you don't forgive, you will develop a root of bitterness and a bitter root will grow bitter fruit. You will become bitter.

Most important of all, you are to forgive because God says so.

> "Bear with each other and forgive whatever grievances you may have against one another. Forgive as the Lord forgave you." (Colossians 3:13)

How to Handle "The Hook"

▶ Imagine right now a hook attached to your collarbone. And imagine all the pain attached to the hook that is a result of the wrong that was done to you.

▶ Ask yourself, *Do I really want to carry all this pain with me for the rest of my life?* The Lord wants you to take the pain from the past and release it into His hands.

▶ Then take the offender off of your emotional hook and place that person onto God's hook. The Lord knows how to deal with your offender. He says …

"It is mine to avenge; I will repay. In due time their foot will slip; their day of disaster is near and their doom rushes upon them." (Deuteronomy 32:35)

PRAYER TO FORGIVE YOUR OFFENDER

"Lord Jesus, thank You for caring about how much my heart has been hurt. You know the pain I have felt because of (list every offense). Right now I release all that pain into Your hands. Thank You, Lord, for dying on the cross for me and extending Your forgiveness to me. As an act of my will, I choose to forgive (name). Right now, I take him off of my emotional hook, and I place him onto Your hook. I refuse all thoughts of revenge. I trust that in Your time and in Your way You will deal with him as You see fit. And Lord, thank You for giving me Your power to forgive so that I can be set free. In Your precious name I pray. Amen."

We may need to go through many bouts of forgiving. Forgiving again and again is just part of the *process of forgiveness*. As we consistently release each recurring thought of an offense, eventually the thoughts will stay away. The process will be complete. The fight will be won. Jesus emphasized the "again and again" nature of forgiveness when He said ...

"If he [your brother] sins against you seven times in a day, and seven times comes back to you and says, 'I repent,' forgive him."
(Luke 17:4)

How to Forgive ... Again

FORBID recurring thoughts of the wrongs to enter your mind. Stop them as soon as they occur. Boldly say to yourself, *I refuse to keep a record of this. I refuse to keep a ledger.*

"[Love] keeps no record of wrongs."
(1 Corinthians 13:5)

OVERCOME the temptation to bring up the matter again. After there has been honest confrontation with the offender and both sides of the situation have been dealt with or if the other person refuses to talk about the problem, let the Holy Spirit do His work of conviction.

"[There is] a time to be silent and a time to speak." (Ecclesiastes 3:7)

Pray this passage: *"Set a guard over my mouth, O Lord; keep watch over the door of my lips."* (Psalm 141:3)

Repeat Scripture in your mind. Allow God's perspective to change your perspective. Allow God's heart to permeate your heart. At times of testing, repeat over and over, "Love covers this wrong. Lord, may I be an expression of Your love. May I reflect Your love that covers over all wrongs."

"Hatred stirs up dissension, but love covers over all wrongs." (Proverbs 10:12)

Give the situation to God. Jesus understands how much you have been wronged. When He was being persecuted, Jesus knew that the heavenly Father would judge justly, in His way, in His time. And you can know the same. Your trial will make you either bitter or better. Say to the Lord, "I put my heart into Your hands. I entrust myself to You. I know You will judge this situation justly." These words were said about Jesus:

"When they hurled their insults at him, he did not retaliate; when he suffered, he made no threats. Instead, he entrusted himself to him who judges justly." (1 Peter 2:23)

Iɴᴛᴇʀᴄᴇᴅᴇ on behalf of your offender. God does not present prayer as an option for you; it is a command. When you have been wronged, pray, "Lord, give me eyes to see him through Your eyes. May I care for her with Your care."

"Bless those who curse you, pray for those who mistreat you." (Luke 6:28)

Vᴀʟᴜᴇ what you can give rather than what you can receive. Pray for God to help you understand the offender's past and how his or her inner pain has contributed to the injury you are now experiencing. Focus on how you might meet some of these inner needs, for it is more blessed to give than to receive.

"In everything I did, I showed you that by this kind of hard work we must help the weak, remembering the words the Lord Jesus himself said: 'It is more blessed to give than to receive.'" (Acts 20:35)

Eхᴛᴇɴᴅ God's grace, mercy, and forgiveness. Forgiveness is a direct expression of both God's grace and God's mercy. Grace is getting what you don't deserve (pardon). Mercy is not getting what you do deserve (punishment). Pray often, "Lord, may my life be an expression of Your grace and an extension of Your mercy."

"The Lord is full of compassion and mercy." (James 5:11)

Following conflict, what keeps your heart from a negative focus? Jesus said, *"Love your enemies."* Impossible! Unrealistic! No way! People can't love their enemies—at least that's the assumption. Yet, the Greek word *agape*, translated "love" in this passage, by definition means "a commitment to seek the highest good of another person."[29] The "highest good" for those who are genuinely *wrong* is that their hearts become genuinely *right*. What can be one major catalyst for this change? Jesus provides the answer:

> "Love your enemies and pray for those who persecute you." (Matthew 5:44)

If you are saying, "but they really aren't enemies," realize that if someone evokes resentment, bitterness, or hatred, that person is an enemy to your spirit. Because praying for your enemy is commanded by Christ, believers should obey this directive and not regard this as optional. And because praying for your enemy protects your heart from bitterness, you should **want** to obey this directive in heart and in deed. One approach is to pray "the fruit of the Spirit" for your offender. And because you are willing to "bless" your enemy, the Bible says that you will inherit a blessing.

> "Do not repay evil with evil or insult with insult, but with blessing, because to this you were called so that you may inherit a blessing." (1 Peter 3:9)

How to Pray for Those Who Hurt You

"The fruit of the Spirit is love, joy, peace, patience, kindness, goodness, faithfulness, gentleness and self-control. Against such things there is no law."
(Galatians 5:22–23)

"*Lord*, I pray that (name) will be filled with *the fruit of love* by becoming fully aware of Your unconditional *love*—and in turn will be able to *love* others.

"*Lord*, I pray that (name) will be filled with *the fruit of joy* because of experiencing Your steady *joy*—and in turn will radiate that inner *joy* to others.

"*Lord*, I pray that (name) will be filled with *the fruit of peace—Your inner peace*—and in turn will have a *peace* that passes all understanding toward others.

"*Lord*, I pray that (name) will be filled with *the fruit of patience* because of experiencing Your *patience*—and in turn will extend that same extraordinary *patience* to others.

"*Lord*, I pray that (name) will be filled with *the fruit of kindness* because of experiencing Your *kindness*—and in turn will extend that same undeserved *kindness* to others.

"*Lord*, I pray that (name) will be filled with *the fruit of goodness* because of experiencing the genuine *goodness* of Jesus—and in turn will reflect the moral *goodness* of Jesus before others.

"*Lord*, I pray that (name) will be filled with *the fruit of faithfulness* because of realizing Your amazing *faithfulness*—and in turn will desire to be *faithful* to You, to Your Word, and to others.

"*Lord*, I pray that (name) will be filled with *the fruit of gentleness* because of experiencing Your *gentleness*—and in turn will be able to be *gentle* with others.

"*Lord*, I pray that (name) will be filled with *the fruit of self-control*—the *control of self* by Christ—and in turn will rely on His *control* for enablement to break out of bondage and to be an example before others.

In the name of Jesus I pray. Amen."

"The wisdom that comes from heaven is first of all pure; then peace-loving, considerate, submissive, full of mercy and good fruit, impartial and sincere."
(James 3:17)

Turning Foes into Friends

Fɪɴᴅ ways to compliment your opposer.

- Look for and express positive character traits that your opposer possesses.

- Don't focus on complimentary externals such as clothes, hair, good looks.

- Express a sincere compliment at an appropriate time. "I've noticed (how effectively you spoke, worked, sang), and I really admire that."

"The mouth of the righteous man utters wisdom, and his tongue speaks what is just." (Psalm 37:30)

Rᴇᴘᴀʏ evil with good toward your opposer.

- Look for and extend acts of kindness.

- Commit to God that you will not act negatively like your opposer.

- Do not talk about your opposer in a demeaning way to others.

"Do not repay anyone evil for evil. Be careful to do what is right in the eyes of everybody." (Romans 12:17)

Iɴᴛᴇʀᴄᴇᴅᴇ in prayer for your opposer.

- Ask God to reveal your opposer's real needs.

- Seek the Lord's perspective on the differences between you and your opposer.

- Commit to praying for your opposer every time that person comes to mind.

"Far be it from me that I should sin against the LORD by failing to pray for you. And I will teach you the way that is good and right." (1 Samuel 12:23)

EMPATHIZE with your opposer.

- Learn about the past hurts and hardships your opposer has experienced.
- Get in touch with your feelings as you think about your own hurts and hardships.
- Allow yourself to feel compassion as you identify with your opposer.

"Rejoice with those who rejoice; mourn with those who mourn." (Romans 12:15)

NURTURE a forgiving heart toward your opposer.

- Realize that you were once a sinner without the love of the Lord.
- Imagine what life was like before you were a true believer.
- Pray for God to give you a willingness to forgive just as He was willing to forgive you.

"When you stand praying, if you hold anything against anyone, forgive him, so that your Father in heaven may forgive you your sins." (Mark 11:25)

DECIDE to love your opposer.

- See yourself as a conduit of God's love.
- Look for tangible ways to express love on a continual basis.

- Keep focusing on "What is the best interest of my opposer"—and then do it.

"Let no debt remain outstanding, except the continuing debt to love one another, for he who loves his fellowman has fulfilled the law." (Romans 13:8)

SEEK to meet the needs of your opposer.

- Reach out—look for what is especially meaningful to your opposer (such as reaching out to one of that person's loved ones).

- Reach out—invite your opposer to attend an event with you that you know that person would like.

- Reach out—take food to your opposer when you hear that person is sick or has lost a loved one.

"If your enemy is hungry, feed him; if he is thirsty, give him something to drink. In doing this, you will heap burning coals on his head." (Romans 12:20)

> *When you are faced with conflict,*
> *passivity is not the real path to peace.*
> *Resolution rests in confronting wrong,*
> *but with a right heart.*
>
> —June Hunt

SCRIPTURES TO MEMORIZE

Am I aware of how **powerful my tongue** is?

*"Death and life are in the **power of the tongue**, and those who love it will eat its fruits."* (Proverbs 18:21, ESV)

Do I sometimes laugh at others, **belittling** them for their faults and failures?

*"Whoever **belittles** his neighbor lacks sense, but a man of understanding remains silent."* (Proverbs 11:12, ESV)

What will help me **accept others** when I see their glaring faults?

*"**Accept one another**, then, just as Christ accepted you, in order to bring praise to God."* (Romans 15:7)

Do I look for ways to **build others up** when they are wrong?

*"Do not let any unwholesome talk come out of your mouths, but only what is helpful for **building others up** according to their needs, that it may benefit those who listen."* (Ephesians 4:29)

How can I know if my heart is **offensive** toward others?

*"Search me, O God, and know my heart; test me and know my anxious thoughts. See if there is any **offensive** way in me, and lead me in the way everlasting."* (Psalm 139:23–24)

What should I **think about** to help me develop positive attitudes?

*"Whatever is true, whatever is noble, whatever is right, whatever is pure, whatever is lovely, whatever is admirable—if anything is excellent or praiseworthy—**think about** such things."* (Philippians 4:8)

Do I see that my unclean words reveal an **unclean** heart?

*"Nothing outside a man can make him 'unclean' by going into him. Rather, it is what comes out of a man that makes him '**unclean**.'"* (Mark 7:15)

Do I see my own sin when I **pass judgment** on others?

*"You, therefore, have no excuse, you who **pass judgment** on someone else, for at whatever point you judge the other, you are condemning yourself, because you who pass judgment do the same things."* (Romans 2:1)

How should I **answer** when others display **anger** toward me?

*"A gentle **answer** turns away wrath, but a harsh word stirs up **anger**."* (Proverbs 15:1)

Am I known by an attitude of pride or **humility**?

*"Everyone who exalts himself will be humbled, and he who **humbles** himself will be exalted."* (Luke 14:11)

Answers to Questions

Suggested answers to the questions on pages 32–37, "Who displays which style of conflict in Scripture?"

Eve: She is an avoider, a weasel. She tried to weasel out of accepting responsibility for her wrong choices by blaming the serpent.

Cain: He is an attacker, a wolf. He became angry when God chastised him regarding his offering.

The Philistines: They are attackers, wolves. They were predators waiting to conquer their prey.

Delilah: She is an attacker, a snake. She accepted a bribe from the Philistines to trap Samson.

Samson: He is an avoider, a chameleon. He told the secret of his strength just to please Delilah.

King Saul: He is an attacker, a wolf. He was jealous of David.

King David: He is an avoider, a turtle. He sought to keep his affair with Bathsheba a secret from her husband, Uriah.

The Pharisees: They are attackers, snakes. They sought to control everyone with laws. They accused Jesus of blasphemy.

Pilate: He is an avoider, a chameleon. He knew that Jesus was innocent, yet condemned Him to death because the crowd insisted that Jesus be crucified.

Judas: He is an attacker, a snake. He betrayed Jesus for thirty pieces of silver.

Martha: She is an attacker, a hornet. She complained to Jesus about her sister Mary.

Peter: He is an avoider, a turtle. He denied ever knowing Jesus.

NOTES

1. *Merriam-Webster Collegiate Dictionary* (2001), s.v. "Conflict"; http://www.m-w.com.

2. *Merriam-Webster*, s.v. "Conflict."

3. Marvin Richardson Vincent, *Word Studies in the New Testament*, vol. 3 (Bellingham, WA: Logos Research Systems, Inc., 2002) 481.

4. *Merriam-Webster*, s.v. "Resolution."

5. *New Oxford Dictionary of English*, electronic ed., (Oxford University Press, 1998); *Merriam-Webster Collegiate Dictionary.* On the differences between resolution and reconciliation see also L. Randolph Lowry and Richard W. Meyers, *Conflict Management and Counseling*, Resources for Christian Counseling, ed. Gary R. Collins, vol. 29 (Waco, TX: Word, 1991), 26–29.

6. G. Brian Jones and Linda Phillips-Jones, *A Fight to the Better End* (Wheaton, IL: Victor, 1989), 16.

7. Jones, *Fight to the Better End*, 16–17.

8. Don Baker, *Restoring Broken Relationships* (Eugene, OR: Harvest House, 1989), 131.

9. Jones, *Fight to the Better End*, 26–28.

10. Cunningham divides the conflict styles into "Attacking" and "Avoidance." Will Cunningham, *How to Enjoy a Family Fight* (Phoenix, AR: Questar, 1988), 148.

11. Cunningham, *How to Enjoy a Family Fight*, 145.

12. Cunningham, *How to Enjoy a Family Fight*, 159–166; Bramson calls this style "the Sherman Tank." Robert M. Bramson, *Coping with Difficult People* (Garden City, NY: Doubleday, 1981), 13.

13. Bramson, *Coping with Difficult People*, 26–29.

14. Bramson, *Coping with Difficult People*, 44–52; Cunningham calls this style of conflict "the Skunk." Cunningham, *How to Enjoy a Family Fight*, 151–58.

15. Cunningham, *How to Enjoy a Family Fight*, 167–176; see also Bramson, *Coping with Difficult People*, 70–73.

16. Bramson, *Coping with Difficult People*, 85–90.

17. Cunningham, *How to Enjoy a Family Fight*, 177–180. Cunningham calls this style "the Chameleon."

18. Lawrence J. Crabb, Jr., *Understanding People: Deep Longings for Relationship*, Ministry Resources Library (Grand Rapids: Zondervan, 1987), 15–16; Robert S. McGee, *The Search for Significance*, 2nd ed. (Houston, TX: Rapha, 1990), 27–30.

19. Terry Hershey, *Intimacy: The Longing of Every Human Heart* (Eugene, OR: Harvest House, 1984), 147–148.

20. Jones, *Fight to the Better End*, 43.

21. William D. Backus, *Telling Each Other the Truth* (Minneapolis, MN: Bethany House, 1985), 106–108.

22. Bramson, *Coping*, 14–25; see also H. Norman Wright, *How to Get Along with Almost Anyone: A Complete Guide to Building Positive Relationships with Family, Friends, Co-workers* (Dallas: Word, 1989), 140–143.

23. Bramson, *Coping with Difficult People*, 29–34.

24. Bramson, *Coping with Difficult People*, 52–64.

25. Bramson, *Coping with Difficult People*, 74–84 and Wright, *How to Get Along with Almost Anyone*, 136–137.

26. Bramson, *Coping with Difficult People*, 90–97.

27. Jones, *Fight to the Better End*, 60; Josh McDowell, *Resolving Conflict* (Pomona, CA: Focus on the Family, 1989), 8, 51–52, 53–54, 59, 60–61.

28. Cunningham, *How to Enjoy a Family Fight*, 123–125, 127–131, 191. McDowell, *Resolving Conflict*, 11.

29. W.E. Vine, Merrill Unger, and William White, editors, *Vine's Complete Expository Dictionary*, s.v. "Love" (New York: Thomas Nelson, 1985).

SELECTED BIBLIOGRAPHY

Backus, William D. *Telling Each Other the Truth.* Minneapolis, MN: Bethany House, 1985.

Baker, Don. *Restoring Broken Relationships.* Eugene, OR: Harvest House, 1989.

Bramson, Robert M. *Coping with Difficult People.* Garden City, NY: Doubleday, 1981.

Crabb, Lawrence J., Jr. and Dan B. Allender. *Encouragement: The Key to Caring.* Grand Rapids: Zondervan, 1984.

Crabb, Lawrence J., Jr. *Understanding People: Deep Longings for Relationship.* Ministry Resources Library. Grand Rapids: Zondervan, 1987.

Cunningham, Will. *How to Enjoy a Family Fight.* Phoenix, AR: Questar, 1988.

Getz, Gene A. *Encouraging One Another.* Wheaton, IL: Victor, 1981.

Hershey, Terry. *Intimacy: The Longing of Every Human Heart.* Eugene, OR: Harvest House, 1984.

Howard, J. Grant. *The Trauma of Transparency: A Biblical Approach to Inter-Personal Communication.* A Critical Concern Book. Portland, OR: Multnomah, 1979.

Hunt, June. *Healing the Hurting Heart: Answers to Real Letters from Real People.* Dallas: Hope For The Heart, 1995.

Hunt, June. *Seeing Yourself Through God's Eyes.* Dallas: Hope For The Heart, 1989.

Jantz, Gregory L. *Healing the Scars of Emotional Abuse*. Grand Rapids: Fleming H. Revell, 1995.

Jones, G. Brian and Linda Phillips-Jones. *A Fight to the Better End*. Wheaton, IL: Victor, 1989.

Lowry, L. Randolph and Richard W. Meyers. *Conflict Management and Counseling*, Resources for Christian Counseling, ed. Gary R. Collins, vol. 29. Waco, TX: Word, 1991.

McGee, Robert S. *The Search for Significance*. 2nd ed. Houston, TX: Rapha, 1990.

VanVonderen, Jeff. *Families Where Grace Is in Place*. Minneapolis, MN: Bethany House, 1992.

Wright, H. Norman. *How to Get Along with Almost Anyone: A Complete Guide to Building Positive Relationships with Family, Friends, Co-workers*. Dallas: Word, 1989.

June Hunt's HOPE FOR THE HEART minibooks are biblically-based, and full of practical advice that is relevant, spiritually-fulfilling and wholesome.

HOPE FOR THE HEART TITLES

Adultery .... ISBN 9781596366848
Alcohol & Drug Abuse .... ISBN 9781596366596
Anger .... ISBN 9781596366411
Codependency .... ISBN 9781596366510
Conflict Resolution .... ISBN 9781596366473
Confrontation .... ISBN 9781596366886
Considering Marriage .... ISBN 9781596366763
Decision Making .... ISBN 9781596366534
Depression .... ISBN 9781596366497
Domestic Violence .... ISBN 9781596366824
Fear .... ISBN 9781596366701
Forgiveness .... ISBN 9781596366435
Friendship .... ISBN 9781596368828
Gambling .... ISBN 9781596366862
Grief .... ISBN 9781596366572
Guilt .... ISBN 9781596366961
Hope .... ISBN 9781596366558
Loneliness .... ISBN 9781596366909
Manipulation .... ISBN 9781596366749
Marriage .... ISBN 9781596368941
Parenting .... ISBN 9781596366725
Reconciliation .... ISBN 9781596368897
Rejection .... ISBN 9781596366787
Self-Worth .... ISBN 9781596366688
Sexual Integrity .... ISBN 9781596366947
Singleness .... ISBN 9781596368774
Stress .... ISBN 9781596368996
Success Through Failure .... ISBN 9781596366923
Suicide Prevention .... ISBN 9781596366800
Verbal & Emotional Abuse .... ISBN 9781596366459

www.aspirepress.com